P9-DVD-147

Protecting
Our Planet

What Can We Do About
GLOBAL WARMING?

Lorijo Metz

PowerKiDS
press.

New York

To Rabecca Collin, who thinks globally and acts locally

Published in 2010 by The Rosen Publishing Group, Inc.
29 East 21st Street, New York, NY 10010

First Edition

Editor: Amelie von Zumbusch
Book Design: Kate Laczynski
Photo Researcher: Jessica Gerweck

Photo Credits: Cover, p. 1 © Dan Guravich/Corbis; back cover graphic © www.istockphoto.com/Jan Rysavy; p. 4 © Lynda Richardson/Corbis; pp. 6, 10, 14, 16, 18 Shutterstock.com; p. 8 Arctic-Images/Getty Images; p. 12 © Peter Beck/Corbis; p. 20 Brent Winebrenner/Lonely Planet Images/ Getty Images.

Library of Congress Cataloging-in-Publication Data

Metz, Lorijo.
 What can we do about global warming? / Lorijo Metz. — 1st ed.
    p. cm. — (Protecting our planet)
 Includes index.
 ISBN 978-1-4042-8079-3 (lib. bdg.) — ISBN 978-1-4358-2479-9 (pbk.) —
ISBN 978-1-4358-2480-5 (6-pack)
 1. Global warming—Juvenile literature. 2. Greenhouse gases—Juvenile literature.
3. Environmental responsibililty—Juvenile literature. I. Title.
 QC981.8.G56M48 2010
 363.738'74—dc22
                                      2008050766

Manufactured in China

CONTENTS

Baby sea turtles break out of eggs laid on beaches. Sadly, the

What Is Global Warming?

Our Earth is home to many beautiful plants and animals. It is just the right **temperature** for these living things to grow and live. However, over the last hundred years, Earth's **average** temperature has begun to rise. This change is called global warming.

Scientists believe global warming is causing problems, such as larger, more powerful storms and rising water in our oceans. Certain plants and animals may be dying because of global warming. Most scientists believe people and the way they live are the leading cause of global warming. Luckily, there are several things we can do to help slow down global warming.

Refineries are factories where oil is turned into gasoline.
They put greenhouse gases into Earth's atmosphere.

What Causes Global Warming?

Greenhouse gases in Earth's **atmosphere** cause global warming. These gases make the atmosphere act like a greenhouse, or a building for growing plants. Greenhouses have glass walls that let in sunlight and trap heat. This keeps greenhouses warm. In the same way, greenhouse gases trap heat near Earth, keeping our planet warm. This is called the greenhouse effect. Without it, Earth would be too cold for living things.

When too much greenhouse gas gets into Earth's atmosphere, it traps too much heat and causes global warming. Today's factories, cars, and power stations produce far more greenhouse gas than people did in the past.

Global warming is causing many glaciers to melt. These scientists are measuring Iceland's Eyjafjallajökull glacier.

Climate Change

Today, global warming is causing climate change. The weather conditions in a place over a long time are that place's climate. For example, the North Pole's climate is cold. Places with different climates are home to different animals. Farmers can grow different crops in different climates, too.

Some changes in Earth's climate are natural. By studying **glacier** ice, scientists have discovered that Earth's climate has changed very slowly over time. However, scientists believe global warming is now causing climate change to happen more quickly. Some animals, such as polar bears, are in danger because Earth's climate is changing too fast for them to **adapt**.

The Italian city of Venice has waterways, called canals. Rising
water caused by global warming is a big problem for Venice.

Why Should You Care?

If you live in a cold climate, the warmer temperatures caused by global warming might sound good. However, if you were a penguin, you might find global warming melting your icy home faster than you could adapt.

About half of all people live near oceans. As global warming causes Earth's glaciers to melt, oceans are rising. This puts animals, including humans, in danger. Today, rising temperatures have already caused flooding and storms that have hurt people and their homes. Towns and cities in low-lying places or along the coast are in the greatest danger of flooding.

DID YOU KNOW?

In the coming years, the people of Tuvalu, an island nation in the Pacific Ocean, will have to leave their homes forever because of flooding and storms.

You can fight global warming by recycling. Many things made from glass, metal, and plastic can be recycled.

How Can You Help?

Energy used to heat and cool our homes produces the greenhouse gases that cause global warming. One way to slow global warming is to **conserve** energy. People can save energy by turning down the heat during winter and wearing more clothes instead. During the summer, you can turn down the air conditioning and use a fan to keep cool. Lights, TVs, and computers use energy, so turn them off whenever possible.

If your family needs a new refrigerator or clothes dryer, remind them to buy the energy-saving kind. Whenever possible, buy **recycled** goods. It takes less energy to make recycled goods than to make new ones.

Transportation, or ways of getting from one place to another, can also produce greenhouse gases. Cars produce the greenhouse gas carbon dioxide. Using transportation that produces less carbon dioxide helps our Earth. Traveling by bus, train, or subway makes less greenhouse gases than riding in a car does. Walking or riding your bike produces no greenhouse gases!

Today, car companies are building cars that use new kinds of energy that produce less greenhouse gases. For example, hybrid electric cars run on both **electricity** and gas. Hydrogen fuel cell cars run on electricity powered by a gas called hydrogen.

DID YOU KNOW?

China's new high-speed train, the Shanghai Maglev Train, is powered by magnetism and electricity. The train produces no greenhouse gases.

Renewable Energy

We can also help slow down global warming by using renewable energy. Renewable energy is energy that comes from natural **resources** that we have an endless supply of, such as wind, sunlight, and water. Renewable energy produces no greenhouse gases.

The Sun produces a large amount of heat and energy. Today, people have learned how to use this energy, called solar power, to heat our water and homes. Wind **turbines** are used to catch power and make electricity. Wind farms, with dozens of wind turbines, produce electricity for many families.

DID YOU KNOW?

People have been using wind power for many years. For example, people used wind power to sail boats along the Nile River in Egypt over 5,000 years ago!

Thick, wet forests, called rain forests, take in lots of carbon dioxide. Sadly, Earth's rain forests are disappearing quickly.

Carbon dioxide is the most plentiful greenhouse gas. When you ride in a car, the car lets out carbon dioxide. Coal and oil burned to heat buildings also produce carbon dioxide. However, nature is here to help!

Oceans and forests are carbon sinks, or places that take in and store carbon dioxide. Oceans are the largest carbon sinks, but forests also take in lots of carbon dioxide. Today, people are cutting down forests around the world. Forests can no longer take in as much carbon dioxide. Therefore, we must plant new trees and take care of the forests we already have.

These wind turbines are in Livermore, California. California makes more renewable energy than any other U.S. state.

Global warming is a worldwide problem. Greenhouse gases produced by one country lead to global warming for everyone. Nations must work together to fight global warming. Developed, or rich, nations, such as the United States, have many cars and factories. These countries produce more greenhouse gas than poorer nations do. Developed countries can fight global warming by conserving energy and changing to renewable energy.

Poorer nations want their people to have better lives. In the past, this has meant having more cars and factories. These nations can fight global warming by building their new factories and power plants to run on renewable energy.

Change Begins with You

Around the world, people are discovering ways to conserve energy. Some states, such as California, Hawaii, and New Jersey, have passed laws to **reduce** greenhouse gases. Japan plans to mark goods to show how much greenhouse gas was produced when the goods were made.

You can help fight global warming, too. Look at how much energy you use every day and try to use less. Talk to your family about conserving energy. Ask your teacher or librarian to help you find books about global warming. Learning about global warming is the first step toward keeping Earth the right temperature for all living things!

GLOSSARY

adapt (uh-DAPT) To change to fit requirements.

atmosphere (AT-muh-sfeer) The gases around an object in space. On Earth this is air.

average (A-vrij) Common or ordinary.

conserve (kun-SERV) To keep something from being wasted or used up.

electricity (ih-lek-TRIH-suh-tee) Power that produces light, heat, or movement.

energy (EH-nur-jee) The power to work or to act.

glacier (GLAY-shur) A large mass of ice.

recycled (ree-SY-kuld) Made from matter that was once used to make something else.

reduce (rih-DOOS) To grow smaller or produce less of something.

resources (REE-sors-ez) Supplies of energy or useful things.

scientists (SY-un-tists) People who study the world.

temperature (TEM-pur-cher) How hot or cold something is.

turbines (TER-bynz) Motors that turn by a flow of water or wind.

INDEX

WEB SITES

Due to the changing nature of Internet links, PowerKids Press has developed an online list of Web sites related to the subject of this book. This site is updated regularly. Please use this link to access the list: www.powerkidslinks.com/ourpl/warming/